CANNIBALISM AND THE COPENHAGEN INTERPRETATION:

A LOVE STORY

poems by

Victoria Woolf Bailey

Finishing Line Press
Georgetown, Kentucky

CANNIBALISM AND THE COPENHAGEN INTERPRETATION:

A LOVE STORY

Copyright © 2022 by Victoria Woolf Bailey
ISBN 978-1-64662-788-2 First Edition
All rights reserved under International and Pan-American Copyright Conventions. No part of this book may be reproduced in any manner whatsoever without written permission from the publisher, except in the case of brief quotations embodied in critical articles and reviews.

ACKNOWLEDGMENTS

Special thanks to the Riverbend Review, a publication of the Henderson campus of the Kentucky Community and Technical College System, who originally published "The Myth of Sisyphus" as well as many of my other poems throughout the years. I am very thankful for their encouragement.

Thanks also go to the members of Green River Writers and to my many teachers, including Kelly Moffett, Mary Ann Samyn, Jane Gentry, and Maurice Manning, among others. I am so grateful for the opportunities I've had be instructed by such fine poets.

Each of the six-line stanzas in these poems was inspired by a different chapter in the book, 1001 IDEAS THAT CHANGED THE WAY WE THINK, edited by Robert Arp, published by Atria Books.

Publisher: Leah Huete de Maines
Editor: Christen Kincaid
Cover Art: Inkberry Images—Victoria Woolf Bailey
Author Photo: Michael Gray, Gray Photography
Cover Design: Elizabeth Maines McCleavy

Order online: www.finishinglinepress.com
also available on amazon.com

Author inquiries and mail orders:
Finishing Line Press
P. O. Box 1626
Georgetown, Kentucky 40324
U. S. A.

Table of Contents

ETERNAL FLUX 1
NUNCHI AND MAXWELL'S DEMON 2
THE MISSING LETTER EFFECT 3
CANNIBALISM AND THE COPENHAGEN INTERPRETATION ... 4
NEURO-LINGUISTIC PROGRAMING 5
MERITOCRACY 6
COUNTERCULTURE 7
PRAGMATISM AND THE SOCIETY OF THE SPECTACLE 8
COMPULSORY EDUCATION 9
THE PSYCHEDELIC EXPERIENCE 10
TALKIES 11
SURREALISM AND ANESTHESIA 12
MOTION AS THE NATURAL STATE OF THINGS. 13
TABULA RASA AND THE FIBONACCI NUMBERS 14
DEFLATIONARY THEORY OF TRUTH 15
CYNICISM AND THE IMPOSSIBLE OBJECT 16
CHAPTER ONE—REVIEW QUESTIONS 17
WIND POWER AND COMEDY 21
THE GOLDEN RATIO 22
THE DRAKE EQUATION 23
PUNCTUATED EQUILIBRIUM 24
MUSICAL INDETERMINACY 25
PHRENOLOGY, UPCYCLING AND THE RADIANT CITY 26
AUTOSUGGESTION 27
ARTISTIC SYMBOLISM 28
CHAPTER TWO—REVIEW QUESTIONS 29
ENCYCLOPEDIA 33
THE FLYNN EFFECT 34

CELL THEORY AND FAMILY THERAPY 35
BIG BROTHER AND THE THEORY OF COMMUNICATIVE
    ACTION 36
ARCHETYPES AND NEWTON'S COLOR WHEEL 37
THE COLD WAR 38
ANTIMATTER AND THE OSCILLATING UNIVERSE 39
THE BEETLE IN THE BOX 40
STRING THEORY 41
CUBISM AND CONTINUAL PROGRESS 42
LOBOTOMY 43
SENSE AND REFERENCE 44
MALE GAZE AND THE GOTHIC IDEAL 45
JAZZ MUSIC 46
PRODUCT PLACEMENT AND ELECTRICITY 47
CHAPTER THREE—REVIEW QUESTIONS 48
FOUNTAIN OF YOUTH 51
PASTEURIZATION 52
THE NATURE OF PERSONAL IDENTITY 53
NEWS FROM NOWHERE 54
NON-JUNK DNA 55
THE MYTH OF SISYPHUS 56
PARADIGM SHIFT 57
WORMHOLES 58
TRIAL BY JURY 59
CHAPTER FOUR—REVIEW QUESTIONS 60
FINAL EXAM 61

For Bruce
Who would I be without you?

CHAPTER ONE

ETERNAL FLUX

They are part of life, the visible
and invisible. I write.
You build an asylum.
Did you think you could contain
the likes of me? Under my coat
I have wings.

You shake your head
and wash in a stream
of new water.
You knew me yesterday.
Did you think you could step
into the same river twice?

Break down the walls.
Make room for my big ideas.
Can't you understand
what I'm seeing?
Don't ask for evidence.
My world is full of wonder.

NUNCHI AND MAXWELL'S DEMON

I imagine a wall
or maybe it's a real wall
made of brick and maybe
there's a door. Maybe
you are knocking. Why
is it so hard for me to give an answer?

We have both held glass,
thrown it against a wall
and watched it shatter.
Will you do the same to me
when you see I am flawed?
I am full of fear.

My questions end
with a mark of finality.
Can you read the meaning
behind my words?
Once I wrote my diary in code.
Maybe I still do.

THE MISSING LETTER EFFECT

Days roll by with moments
missed in the retelling.
Sometimes I am silent,
a fish swimming under ice.
How much is hidden
in my lack of words?

CANNIBALISM AND THE COPENHAGEN INTERPRETATION

You watch as I light the flame.
I will leave pots and pans in the sink.
I will feed on your flesh and complain
about the bones. Was I made for this?
I savor the taste of your temples,
the brow that furrows in my defense.

I am the cat who demands
food. I am the cat who howls
at the neighbor's door.
What would you expect
from someone like me? I purr,
I growl. You know how it is.

I will give you steam or ice.
Do you understand how hard
it is for me to choose?
Tomorrow will be different,
and the day after that,
and the day after that.

NEURO-LINGUISTIC PROGRAMING

You are not my type,
tie and suit, the ever-present
khakis, and here I am
in the midst of a struggle
you have never known.
Will we both have to change?

The thrill of the unknown,
the search for what may or may not
exist, spurs us on. If I stick
out my thumb and run
you would track me down.
Why is it you care so much?

MERITOCRACY

I see you exit the elevator,
legal pad in hand.
I am surviving a dead-end job,
poor, wet and dirty.
How could you ever love
someone like me?

I listen to you speak on the phone
and admire your confidence.
I have always avoided making calls.
Will you help me become
a better person?
I will give lessons in return.

COUNTERCULTURE

I see you watching me
with eyes full of sincerity.
I have never known you to lie.
I ask so many questions.
How do I know what is true?
Every day is a struggle.

I reject your advances.
Your world is your world,
not mine. But soon I begin to dream
and accept that I might survive
on the fringes of the unfamiliar.
How long will I hide in the shadows?

PRAGMATISM AND THE SOCIETY OF THE SPECTACLE

I stand in front of you,
a vision of loveliness
you must possess.
But rain has fallen
and I am soaked to the skin.
What is it you are seeing?

You can describe my eyes,
that unique color with a circle
of gold, admire my padded frame.
But why do you love me?
Some things are easy to see,
some questions hard to answer.

Words are not enough.
I want to watch you work,
see how you mold and fire
the clay of my world.
Will there always be bread
rising? Feed me.

COMPULSORY EDUCATION

You have told me about the rain.
We have talked about floods,
seen the naked roots of trees
on the banks of the river.
But what do you know of pain?
I will never again go hungry.

I have learned too many lessons.
What can you teach me?
I will open your book and study
late into the night.
Show me what I need to know.
Make it easy.

THE PSYCHEDELIC EXPERIENCE

In its glory the world has vanished
into the daily tasks of living.
Will you show me more?
Blue that is more than blue,
water that swirls on its way
to steam and hardens into ice.

Flowers fade, candy
is consumed. What conclusion
am I supposed to draw
from such generosity?
There's so little logic in love.
You won me with children's shoes.

TALKIES

We are both old masters
covered with the brushstrokes
of our separate lives.
What use is it to debate
the politics of privilege?
I bristle at your old friends.

I struggle to add
a soundtrack to the silence.
When we slow dance in the kitchen
and I sing the words I know by heart,
will this one event
change our world?

SURREALISM AND ANESTHESIA

My thoughts are as fragile as blown glass.
You worry I will shatter and break.
How can you tell the difference
between pleasure and pain?
They both light up the screen
on the doctor's machine.

I will throw off these shackles.
I will dream what I will dream.
When my imagination
is unleashed will you be trapped
in the dome of my desire?
Life is full of contradictions.

I have run through a field
of poppies, inhaled the gas
of laughter, cried against
your chest. Why did I think
you could make it all better?
You wield an exquisite sword.

MOTION AS THE NATURAL STATE OF THINGS

The world is spinning
but we feel nothing.
How fast are we moving?
Hair becomes thinner,
long strands left in the sink.
Everything is changing.

The past breaks through
the surface. I worry.
I am running late.
Why am I so afraid?
I fear a remembered voice
accusing, spewing threats.

So much is happening
unseen. What is it
I am trying to tell you? Stars
speak with long, slow voices.
Maybe I am invisible.
Maybe you are moving too fast.

TABULA RASA AND THE FIBONACCI NUMBERS

Who can erase the past
with its tearful hieroglyphics?
I will not wear white or pretend
I have lived alone and you,
you hear an echo
where no one has spoken.

Together we equal the sum
of two parts or something greater?
Even the flowers in the field
know the answer, petals aligned
in the proper sequence. Alone,
I am rare as a four-leaf clover.

DEFLATIONARY THEORY OF TRUTH

I can explain the color blue
and how it fills this cavern.
You can inch your way
into my mind, examine each crevice.
But how will you ever understand?
You have always been blind.

You have spoken of love.
There is nothing for me
to say. Here I stand
waiting for the concrete to dry
and here my feet will stay,
unmovable. Are you listening?

CYNICISM AND THE IMPOSSIBLE OBJECT

The veil is gone.
The cake has been eaten.
How long will it take us
to see with new eyes?
The world insists
we live in its midst.

Hormones surge and neurons
fire in our coming together.
Steam locomotives whistle
as they run down the track.
Beyond the darkened tunnel,
is there something more?

Is our love nothing
but an endless staircase,
a line drawing of hearts and flowers?
We feel the things we feel.
Maybe it's an illusion.
Maybe it isn't real.

CHAPTER ONE—REVIEW QUESTIONS

1) What is it I am trying to tell you?
2) Can you read the meaning behind my words?
3) Do you understand how hard it is for me to choose?
4) Why am I so afraid?
5) How do I know what is true?
6) Why is it you care so much?

CHAPTER TWO

WIND POWER AND COMEDY

Back in the day we were young
lovers, we were never young lovers.
Each of our pasts can be mined
for material. I stand up and announce
the secret of life. You laugh.
Is that all it takes to make you happy?

There is something invisible
in the air between us.
The leaves, the clouds,
watch how they move.
Why are you amazed
when I know your thoughts?

You bark and I meow.
How will we ever learn
to speak the same language?
Our communication may be difficult
but I have no problem
understanding your needs.

THE GOLDEN RATIO

We have combined the best
of your world and mine,
transferred hard experience
onto the white tablet
of our shared life.
Do we now think alike?

You say yes, I say no.
I worry. Where
are the gongs, whistles
and bells? I have learned
to proceed with caution.
I am no longer green.

I am not perfect. My face
is not that of the Mona Lisa.
I am irrational. But still
you see me as beautiful.
I will never understand.
How can love be infinite?

THE DRAKE EQUATION

Above us there are many worlds
but only one in ten million will speak.
What do you make of my preoccupation
with things that can never be known?
You understand the math.
Maybe I am a fool.

I have discovered
the meaning of ordinary,
the day-by-day washing
of clothes and dishes.
Will you share in the art
I am creating?

PUNCTUATED EQUILIBRIUM

It's all too complicated,
this world of ours with its
bills and endless appointments.
What is the formula
for happiness and how
will we ever find it?

We wait for a change,
a knock on the door,
a graduation. Sometimes
we see it coming, sometimes
we don't. How can life
be so unpredictable?

We see it all around us,
the evidence of love
gone wrong. We hear
so many one-sided stories.
Is no one immune
from anger and hurt?

MUSICAL INDETERMINACY

Our lives are a process.
We look for instructions
and definitions. Who will lead
and who will follow across
this imaginary landscape?
The world is full of ambient noise.

We lay out our land
and our lives. Seven sit
at a table with eight chairs.
Have we managed to create
something beautiful?
There is little to spare.

We draw our plans.
We shift our weight.
We attempt to do
what no one has done.
Can love overcome friction?
Everyone says we are destined to fail.

PHRENOLOGY, UPCYCLING AND THE RADIANT CITY

We drive through mud,
and a hole we call
the moat, in a car covered
with dents. We buy
designer clothes, slightly worn.
Are these the things that define us?

Once there were plans,
an idea we embraced,
but our hammers grew rusty
as we waited on Utopia
to rise. Why were we so afraid
to listen to the voice of reality?

We have set our sights
higher than smashing cans
or paving a new path
with broken bricks of the past.
Where do we go from here?
It's hard to imagine prosperity.

AUTOSUGGESTION

You are mine
and I have become yours.
You wanted an anchor.
I have gained a ship.
Is the weight of my iron
worth what you paid?

I will walk the wire
while you hold the net.
I will hide in the closet
until you coax me out.
How would I survive
without such loving care?

ARTISTIC SYMBOLISM

An explosion of red apples
on an overburdened tree.
A splash of blue, the dark
outline of an imagined world.
Do we share the same dream
of green fields and an abundant harvest?

We wrap ourselves
in a package tied
with the rough twine
of endless work.
What will we find
when we unloose the bow?

CHAPTER TWO—REVIEW QUESTIONS

1)   Where are the gongs, whistles and bells?
2)   How will we ever learn to speak the same language?
3)   Can love overcome friction?
4)   Is no one immune from anger and hurt?
5)   Where do we go from here?
6)   Will you share in the art I am creating?

CHAPTER THREE

ENCYCLOPEDIA

I have learned to sign
a new name and have moved
from the back of the line
to the front. Did you picture
your love changing my life
in so many ways?

In pictures and files and paper
we will link our history together.
We will write our own book
in ten thousand ways.
But will anyone care
about the sum of our knowledge?

THE FLYNN EFFECT

I remember with regret
those wild days,
how we went off course.
Have we become smarter?
Maybe we have grown
or maybe the world has changed.

We live in the chaos
of competing desires,
two melodies, five tunes
playing at once. Can you hear
me singing through the sound
of this symphony?

CELL THEORY AND FAMILY THERAPY

We are two cells in one body
communicating in currents
and the complexity of chemicals.
Is there fire in the gap between us?
Tell me and I will tell you.
There is nowhere to hide.

Deep inside there are reasons.
How could it be otherwise?
Scientists point to glands
and the chemicals created
as if we are nothing
but bowls of warming stew.

At the kitchen table
we are not alone.
We have never been alone.
How can so many add up to one?
The curtain has been lifted.
Let the drama begin.

BIG BROTHER AND THE THEORY OF COMMUNICATIVE ACTION

We build our home
like a stage, recite our lines,
fly like starlings.
Is this what it means
to be a family, to swim
like a school of fish?

Surrounded by youthful curiosity,
we have learned to be quiet
in the dark. How will our children
remember us? They watch
our every move. We are old
and outnumbered.

We are surrounded
by the sounds of bickering,
the energy of young foolishness.
How did this happen?
We made a promise and now—
the great performance.

ARCHETYPES AND NEWTON'S COLOR WHEEL

I will not imitate my mother,
nor you, your father.
But how will we ever find
our own way of being?
You watch sports and grunt.
My room is always cluttered.

Side by side our days swing, each gear
and pulley inching us toward another.
You push and I pull.
Time carries us forward.
One hand alone can change nothing.
Have we been trapped or set free?

We stand on opposite
ends of the spectrum
with different wavelengths
and hues. Watch how fast I can spin.
What faint, anonymous color
will result from our union?

THE COLD WAR

Have you learned to sharpen flint
or only your face?
So much depends on the angle,
the way you hammer the edges.
I admire your crude attempts
and dream of a life of comfort.

Old-fashioned weapons
were designed to kill one at a time.
Will you push the button
and annihilate us both?
We fix each other
and hold a hard stare.

ANTIMATTER AND THE OSCILLATING UNIVERSE

You search through a trunk
full of years gone by,
papers hidden away.
Why are you so curious?
Ask me a question
if you want to know.

I consider and reconsider
the possibilities, how easy
it would be to explode.
There is nothing to stop us.
How hard would it be
to change our course?

It took so long to discover
the truth. We are two dominoes
standing on edge. If we collide
will we annihilate our world?
Will we cease to exist?
Please, please be careful.

THE BEETLE IN THE BOX

Even when I am lazy and mad
you treat me like a goddess.
Do you see through my veil?
There is nothing here
but obscure logic. Maybe
ignorance is a good friend.

I speak and you listen.
I worry. How can you ever
understand? My words
mean nothing.
You will never comprehend
the limits of my world.

STRING THEORY

Our lives have been stuffed
into a package, two forces
vibrating, incompatible, tied
with a thin ribbon. Does our love
have many dimensions?
We have always gone in circles.

We are a chord, a chorus
of chants, a complex braid
twisted from the strands
of these many years.
Can you hear
the difference in our voices?

CUBISM AND CONTINUAL PROGRESS

Look at us, full of angles
and the jaded perspective
of another union.
How can we put the past
and the blind future
into some kind of order?

In my garden I've created
a rainbow and still
I search for more.
Will you change
the color of my mind?
I am tired of wearing black.

We believe every day
and year will be better.
Are we closer to perfection
or are we fooling ourselves?
Now, another friend has fallen.
Maybe we should replace our gutters.

LOBOTOMY

We will trudge toward
the goal, the grave
of all our deficiencies.
Will your love bring
fulfillment or an end
to my illusions?

I will fight you off
but you will win.
The ice pick
will have its way.
Are you ready
to face the results?

The change comes slowly
like the hands of a clock
moving. How did the past
bring us to this place?
Look out the window.
The sky is no longer blue.

SENSE AND REFERENCE

I see the morning star
and call the light day.
You observe the first
glowing object in the evening.
How were we to know
it was all the same?

You mark your time by the sun
with the falling of shadows
and marvel at their perfection.
Why should I care?
Tomorrow will draw lines
on both our faces.

MALE GAZE AND THE GOTHIC IDEAL

I am pleasing to your eyes,
a heroine in the film
of your life, the sweet rescuer.
But we argue. What is my role
in this great narrative
and what is yours?

We have come so far. Each day
with its own meaning slides
into the next. How
will the years change us?
I will put in writing,
all but what lies ahead.

I will walk the halls
of the castle you have built
admiring arches and stained glass.
Come now, I invite you
into the world I have made.
Can you imagine infinity?

JAZZ MUSIC

The marching bands abandon
their drums. I tap my feet,
changing the blues with my
offbeat style. I am restless.
Do you understand the challenge
of dancing to an unknown rhythm?

The wrinkles of a hard woman
could easily have formed
around my mouth and the eyes
that have seen too much.
How did you manage
to bring new life to an old face?

PRODUCT PLACEMENT AND ELECTRICITY

We have hung your name
on signs, jingled it
into the collective mind,
hammered it into history.
How did I get so lucky?
Your name is also mine.

We have become a powerful force,
lives brightened and changed
by the power of our God.
What is it that flows beneath
the workings of this great machine?
Touch me and I will glow.

CHAPTER THREE—REVIEW QUESTIONS

1) Will your love bring fulfillment or an end to my illusions?
2) Do you understand the challenge of dancing to an unknown rhythm?
3) How did the past bring us to this place?
4) Can you hear me singing through the sound of this symphony?
5) How can so many add up to one?
6) Did you picture your love changing my life in so many ways?

CHAPTER FOUR

FOUNTAIN OF YOUTH

You swim in circles
while I kick and tread water.
Time gets shorter
as the world winds toward winter.
Will we ever forget the days
we skinny-dipped in the summer sun?

PASTEURIZATION

I will not disguise
the gray in my hair,
the wrinkles, the new ones
I earn each day.
Would you rather
I wore a mask?

I have spent my hours, shovel in hand,
have fed you the fruit of my labor.
Am I overworked
in this lonely paradise?
There are two seasons here—
grass that grows, and winter for rest.

How can we be safe
from the seeds
of slow spoilage?
There is more to heat
than flame and fire.
Then, there is less.

THE NATURE OF PERSONAL IDENTITY

It takes time to sift
through my endless ideas.
What is the true nature of love?
You are quick with puns.
Some go over my head.
Some are unanswered riddles.

We each have invisible roads
we have traveled,
memories unknown to the other.
If I lost my teeth and hair
would you still love me?
Some things I will never understand.

NEWS FROM NOWHERE

We have fashioned a good place
with trees and vines,
nuts and sweet berries.
But in the middle of paradise
we battle grass and weeds.
What happened to Utopia?

You have begun to speak
more loudly. I am the one
who must read the fine print.
Do you remember
how it used to be
before our world changed?

NON-JUNK DNA

There are moments we remember
and many more we have swept
into the dustpan of forgotten days.
Did we really think time
was endless? Every Tuesday
I hear the clinking of cans.

We stand together in the garden
marveling at our perfection.
Who are we fooling?
I wilt and fade like a flower
while flakes of paint
fall from your façade.

THE MYTH OF SISYPHUS

It's hard to see planets
above the lights of the city.
Once we watched the stars
flicker, so much spread
before us. How could we know
so much would change?

The clearing we cut
in the upper field is gone,
the paths where we picked
blackberries now impassable.
How could we know our work
would all be undone?

We have waited
for generations beyond
what we have created
but our desire is selfish.
When will we learn
to leave well enough alone?

PARADIGM SHIFT

We have moved our lives
from the wild garden
of our imagination
to the civilized convenience
of another world. When
did our dream become unworkable?

That long gravel driveway
and the isolation we once hailed
as privacy are gone. We hold each other
in amazement. Were we never told,
after old dreams wither and die,
a new life would bloom?

WORMHOLES

We dream of what might be
possible but are not prepared
for what we will find
at the end of this long tunnel
of time. How could our lives
pass so quickly?

You are my castle
in the sand. And life,
this life we live, is a wave.
If you were gone,
what would be left?
Broken shells litter the beach.

I have so many questions.
Could our lives be an experiment,
our movement through the years
like a song played in two keys
we recognize as one?
There are many kinds of music.

TRIAL BY JURY

Under a sky full of stars
we walk together, unable to see
all that is above.
How can we ever understand
what really exists
or what lies beyond?

Someday one of us will be left
alone in a blizzard of grief.
Do lonely hearts freeze
and harden or do they
blossom in a world of memories?
Our garden is full of perennials.

If our hearts are broken,
of what crime are we guilty?
We must face the facts.
Salmon swimming upstream
are eaten by bears.
There are no guarantees.

CHAPTER FOUR—REVIEW QUESTIONS

1) How could our lives pass so quickly?
2) When did our dream become unworkable?
3) Do you remember how it used to be before our world changed?
4) If you were gone, what would be left?
5) Do lonely hearts freeze and harden or do they blossom in a world of memories?
6) Will we ever forget the days we skinny-dipped in the summer sun?

FINAL EXAM

True or False:

1) I am not perfect.
2) There is something invisible in the air between us.
3) One hand alone can change nothing.
4) Life is full of contradictions.
5) You wanted an anchor.
6) There is nothing here but obscure logic.
7) Tomorrow will draw lines on both our faces.

Multiple Choice:

1) Why are you amazed when I know your thoughts?
   a. You bark and I meow.
   b. I am irrational.
   c. You understand the math.
   d. It's all too complicated.
   e. All of the above

2) What would you expect from someone like me?
   a. I will leave pots and pans in the sink.
   b. My world is full of wonder.
   c. I will dream what I will dream.
   d. I am rare as a four-leaf clover.
   e. All of the above

3) What is the true nature of love?
   a. There is more to heat than flame and fire.
   b. You have begun to speak more loudly.
   c. There are no guarantees.
   d. Our garden is full of perennials.
   e. All of the above

Essay Questions:

1) Why can you not step into the same river twice?
2) Explain the significance of "a knock on the door."
3) What is it that flows beneath the workings of this great machine?

Extra Credit:

1) How could you ever love someone like me?
2) What happened to Utopia?

Victoria Woolf Bailey began writing poetry in her teens but never had the good sense to give it up. While studying English and Journalism in college she spent four summers traveling all over the country by herself on a Greyhound bus. She attended mountain climbing school in New Mexico and hitchhiked coast to coast. It was the seventies.

After years of traveling and living in eight different states, she finally found the home of her dreams in a small town in rural Kentucky.

In 2012 she won the Accents Publishing Short Poem Award from the Kentucky State Poetry Society as well as Honorable Mention in the Carnegie Center for Literacy and Learning's Next Great Writers contest. Her work has been published in a number of journals including, *The Heartland Review, Still: The Journal, The Tipton Poetry Journal, Kudzu* and *Pegasus* as well as the Motif 3 anthology *All the Livelong Day* published by MotesBooks. Her first chapbook *Dragging Gunter's Chain* was published in 2014 by Finishing Line Press.

www.ingramcontent.com/pod-product-compliance
Lightning Source LLC
Chambersburg PA
CBHW031356160426
42813CB00082B/408